W9-CEO-645

# 20 Answers

## The Sacraments

Fr. Mike Driscoll

Catholic
Answers
Press

*20 Answers: The Sacraments*
**Fr. Mike Driscoll**
© 2016 Catholic Answers

All rights reserved. Except for quotations, no part of this book may be reproduced or transmitted in any form or by any means, electronic or mechanical, including photocopying, recording, uploading to the Internet, or by any information storage and retrieval system, without written permission from the publisher.

Published by Catholic Answers, Inc.
2020 Gillespie Way
El Cajon, California 92020
1-888-291-8000 orders
619-387-0042 fax
catholic.com

Printed in the United States of America

978-1-68357-017-2
978-1-68357-018-9 Kindle
978-1-68357-019-6 ePub

# Introduction

*A sacrament is an outward sign instituted by Christ to give grace.*

This line appeared in the 1885 *Baltimore Catechism* and was the standard definition memorized by Catholic children for the next eighty years. It is still taught by many Catholic parents, school teachers, and adult education instructors. The fact that it was memorized does not mean it was left unexplained; the *Baltimore Catechism* had many further questions and answers describing how the outward signs are performed, where in Scripture Christ is seen to institute them, and what is meant by grace.

Christ is the Word made flesh, God the Son who came into the world in a physical body. Though he also ascended into heaven in his resurrected body, he is still present in physical form in the sacraments. These strongest channels of God's grace enable the faithful to love God and neighbor as Jesus commanded. By keeping the sacraments at the center of our lives, we can know, love, and serve God in this world and one day be happy with him forever in heaven.

## 1. What is a sacrament?

As the *Compendium of the Catechism of the Catholic*

*Church* puts it, sacraments are "efficacious signs of grace perceptible to the senses." They were "instituted by Christ and entrusted to the Church," and through them "divine life is bestowed on us" (*Compendium* 224).

The sacraments are *perceptible to the senses*, meaning they have an external aspect that can be seen, heard, touched, tasted, or smelled. As *efficacious signs of grace*, they really confer the grace they signify. A red light is a sign telling drivers to stop their cars, but it does not cause cars to stop; the drivers themselves must do that. Sacraments are signs that God's grace is being given, but they also give the grace of which they are signs.

The sacraments were *instituted by Christ and entrusted to the Church*. Although some are described in more detail than others, references to all of the sacraments can be found in the New Testament. Jesus entrusted the sacraments to the Church to preserve and administer them as well as to safeguard them. The Church does not have the authority to add more sacraments, abolish any of those that exist, or change the essence of the seven that Jesus instituted. In recent years we have seen examples of these limitations. The Church has stated that it does not have the authority to ordain women to the priesthood; that two men or two women going through a ceremony mimicking marriage does not constitute the sacrament of matrimony; and that priests do not have the ability to change rice cakes into the body of Christ.[1]

## 2. How do sacraments work?

Sacraments can be studied in a way common to classical philosophy, which is to look at the *four causes*: material, formal, efficient, and final. For example, if an artist makes a statue, the material cause is the block of marble he used, the formal cause is the shape of the statue, the efficient cause is the artist, and the final cause is the purpose he had in mind for the statue.

In regard to the sacraments, the *final cause*, or *purpose* for which Jesus instituted them, is to give grace. There are two types of grace given in the sacraments: sanctifying grace and sacramental grace. Sanctifying grace is a gift from God that gives human beings a share in his life: it is God's life in the soul (*Compendium* 423). This grace is the same in all of the sacraments. Sacramental grace is a gift from God that is proper to the sacrament in which it is given; each sacrament gives us a different gift from God (*Compendium* 424).

In the sacraments, the *material cause*, or *matter*, is the aspect that is perceptible to the senses: for example, the water in baptism, and the bread and wine in the Eucharist. The Church has authority over the matter of each sacrament, but it cannot extend the matter in ways that Jesus limited it, not only in Scripture but through Sacred Tradition. For example, though the Bible does not explicitly state that the sacrament of confirmation requires anointing with oil, that has been part of Church Tradition since the beginning, and it cannot be changed to an anointing with water.

The *formal cause*, or *form* of a sacrament, is the spoken words that cause the grace to be conferred. Because Jesus did not explicitly state the words to be used for all of the sacraments, in those cases the Church has the authority to determine what those words are. Furthermore, Jesus spoke Hebrew and Aramaic, but from the beginning of the Church different languages were used for the sacraments, and in order for them to be handed down through time and place, the Church authorizes the words to be used in different languages.

The *efficient cause* of a sacrament is the *minister* who brings together the matter and form, causing the sacrament to take place and God's grace to be given. For example, in baptism he pours the water and says the words, and the sacrament takes place; original sin is wiped away and God's grace is given to the person receiving it. As with matter and form, based on how Jesus and the apostles instituted and passed on each sacrament, the Church determines who is capable of being a minister to confer it. Some sacraments have an *ordinary minister* (for ordinary circumstances) and an *extraordinary minister* (for extraordinary circumstances).

### 3. Why do we have sacraments?

At first it may seem like sacraments are unnecessary. If

God's grace "justifies" or "saves" people, then why do Christians need to receive more grace through sacraments? If his grace is purely a gift, then how can we do something, like receiving sacraments, to get this gift?

Sacraments are not means of earning God's grace; his grace is a gift, and sacraments do not make us deserving of it. Rather, sacraments are part of our covenant with Jesus: he promised that if we do certain things, he will give us the gift of his grace, and thereby the gift of salvation. For example, Jesus taught that the gift of his grace is given through baptism: "Truly, truly, I say to you, unless one is born of water and the Spirit, he cannot enter the kingdom of God" (John 3:5). Similarly, people become his disciples through baptism: "Go therefore and make disciples of all nations, baptizing them in the name of the Father and of the Son and of the Holy Spirit" (Matt. 28:19). Jesus told his disciples to make disciples by baptizing and that he would give the Holy Spirit to those who are baptized. It is through this sacrament that people first receive his life, his grace.

The reason there are additional sacraments is to increase this gift of grace, or to restore it when it is lost completely. Some Christians dispute that grace can be lost, believing that once we're saved, we're always saved. This contradicts what Jesus said: that after accepting him as Lord and Savior, people can still reject him through their sins. "Awake, and strengthen what remains and is on the point of death, for I have not found your works perfect in the sight of my God. Remember then what you received and heard; keep that, and repent" (Rev. 3:2–3; cf. Matt. 7:21–23; 1 Cor. 4:3–5; 1 John 1:8–10; Rev. 2:1–3:22).

The good news is that the more sanctifying grace people have in their souls—the stronger the life of Christ is within them—the better they are able to avoid sins, especially mortal sins. Recall that the sacraments give two kinds of grace: sanctifying and sacramental. Sanctifying grace is God's life in people: it literally sanctifies them—makes them holy—and helps them to follow God's laws. Therefore, by giving sanctifying grace to souls, sacraments help people to avoid committing mortal sins.

Furthermore, sacramental grace helps people in a way specific to the particular sacrament is a gift from God that gives grace for a specific need, whether it be receiving grace for the first time (baptism), the grace to be a husband/wife (matrimony), or the grace to suffer serious illness (anointing of the sick). When people commit mortal sins, though they cannot be baptized again, Jesus gave the sacrament of penance to restore his life to their souls: "And when he had said this, he breathed on them, and said to them, 'Receive the Holy Spirit. If you forgive the sins of any, they are forgiven; if you retain the sins of any, they are retained'" (John 20:22). Baptism and penance have traditionally been called *sacraments of the dead*, not because they are given to people who have died, but because they are given to people in whom God's life has been driven out by deadly sin.

## 4. How can words and material objects give God's grace?

God is eternal: he is outside of time, he has no beginning and no end. As described in the very beginning of the Bible, he created the universe and everything in it by his word, by willing it all to be. But creation does not just exist as a neutral construct. Because it is conceived, created, and kept in existence by God, it is good in itself; the very existence of God's creation glorifies him. This is seen in the cry of the Seraphim heard by the prophet Isaiah: "Holy, holy, holy, the Lord God of hosts, all the earth is full of his glory!" (Isa. 6:3). Similarly, the young men in the book of the prophet Daniel sang a litany of all creation glorifying God: "Bless the Lord, all you works of the Lord, praise and exalt him above all forever" (Dan. 3:57). St. Francis of Assisi's well-known *Canticle of the Sun* is another prayer that praises God for the glory of his creation: "To you alone, Most High, do they belong, and no man is worthy to mention your name. Be praised, my Lord, through all your creatures." Clearly, God is glorified by the material world he created.

In the womb of the Blessed Virgin Mary, God the Son—the same Word of God through whom the world was created (John 1:3)—became part of his own creation: "And the Word became flesh and dwelt among us, full of grace and truth; we have beheld his glory, glory as of the only Son from the Father" (John 1:14). The universe changed at this point: God's material creation no longer simply showed his glory; rather, God himself became part of that creation. God the Son endowed matter with the ability to give his grace, his life. Jesus' flesh—his words and his touch—healed physical ailments and raised the dead. Greatest of all, when he suffered and died on the cross, his flesh became the source of salvation for mankind: "'And I, when I am lifted up from the earth, will draw all men to myself.' He said this to show by what death he was to die" (John 12:32–33).

If Jesus lived and died in Israel 2,000 years ago, how does his life, his grace, reach people throughout the world and throughout the centuries? By making that creation a channel of his grace. In order to extend his grace throughout time and throughout the world, Jesus commissioned the ministers of his Church to administer the sacraments:

> And Jesus came and said to them, "All authority in heaven and on earth has been given to me. Go therefore and make disciples of all nations, baptizing them in the name of the Father and of the Son and of the Holy Spirit" (Matt. 28:18–19).

And he took bread, and when he had given thanks he broke it and gave it to them, saying, "This is my body, which is given for you. Do this in remembrance of me" (Luke 22:19).

He breathed on them, and said to them, "Receive the Holy Spirit. If you forgive the sins of any, they are forgiven; if you retain the sins of any, they are retained" (John 20:22–23).

Sacraments are not magic tricks, but they do have power in themselves. They are said to have their effect *ex opera operato*, which may be translated *by the work done*. This means that when a sacrament is performed according to the ritual of the Church, its intended effect is not dependent on the person administering it; it is effective on its own. For example, when people go to confession, if they confess their sins honestly and sincerely ask forgiveness, their sins are forgiven when the priest says the proper words from the Rite of Penance. The priest may be a great saint or a great sinner, but that does not affect the power of the sacrament. The sins are forgiven *by the work done*. All seven sacraments work in this way.

## 5. What is the difference between sacraments and sacramentals?

By the authority Christ gave it, the Church has also

instituted *sacramentals*, which are signs that give his grace in a way that resembles the sacraments (*Catechism of the Catholic Church* (CCC) 1667–1673). By the power of prayer, the sign of the cross, and holy water, ministers of the Church sanctify the whole range of Christian life by blessing persons, occasions, and objects. There are blessings for homes, vehicles, tools, land, and produce; indeed, "there is scarcely any proper use of material things which cannot be thus directed toward the sanctification of men and the praise of God" (CCC 1670). The blessing of sacramentals is often reserved to clergy (bishops, priests, and deacons), but there are some sacramentals that are performed by all members of the Church, such as making the sign of the cross, sprinkling holy water, and anointing with blessed oil: "Sacramentals do not confer the grace of the Holy Spirit in the way that the sacraments do, but by the Church's prayer they prepare us to receive grace and dispose us to cooperate with it" (CCC 1670). Whereas sacraments are effective *ex opera operato*, by the work done, sacramentals are effective *ex opere operantis Ecclesiae*, by the action of the Church (see Pius XII, *Mediator Dei*, n. 27, Nov. 20, 1947).

Some sacramentals are actions alone, such as the sign of the cross, the blessing of a person, or the Rite of Exorcism; these may be called *transitory* sacramentals. Others may be called *permanent* sacramentals: they are objects that are given spiritual power through prayer of the Church. For example, when water is blessed using the

*Rituale Romanum*, the priest says, "May you be a purified water, empowered to drive afar all power of the enemy, in fact, to root out and banish the enemy himself, along with his fallen angels." The water thus becomes a permanent sacramental: the prayerful request of the Church is asked for every place it is sprinkled. In regard to a permanent sacramental the object is blessed regardless of the state of the priest's soul: for example, even a priest in a state of mortal sin may effectively do the blessing of holy water. But when a priest performs a transitory sacramental such as blessing a sick person or performing the Rite of Exorcism, its effectiveness may, to some degree, depend upon the holiness (or sinfulness) of the priest (see James 5:16).

## 6. What does it mean for a sacrament to be "valid" and "licit"?

In the *Code of Canon Law* (CIC, for *Codex Iuris Canonici*), the official document that regulates ecclesial matters, the Church prescribes for each sacrament what is valid, what is licit, and who is an ordinary or extraordinary minister.

A *valid* sacrament is one that has the necessary matter, form, minister, and intention for the sacrament to take place. Without these elements, the ceremony is invalid, and the sacrament does not actually take place. According to the *Code*, "Since the sacraments are the same for the whole Church and belong to the divine deposit, it is only for the supreme authority of the Church to approve or define the requirements for their validity" (CIC 841). Priests and the other ministers have to follow the directives that the Church requires in order for sacraments to be valid.

For example, for the valid consecration of bread and wine at Mass, the Church requires that the bread be made of wheat and the wine of grapes; the words of consecration must be spoken as provided in the missal ("This is my body. . . . This is the chalice of my blood"); the minister must be an ordained priest; and he must have at least the implicit intention of performing the consecration. If these conditions are not met—if the priest used bread or wine made of other ingredients, if he changed the words of consecration, etc.—then the consecration is invalid, and the bread and wine do not become body and blood of Christ.

Given that a sacrament has been done validly, i.e. that it has actually taken place, it is also important that it be *licit*, which means it is done lawfully. For example, Church law states that in ordinary circumstances, a cleric (deacon, priest, or bishop) is to perform a baptism, but in case of necessity anyone may do so. What if a lay person attempts a baptism when it is not a case of necessity? If the matter, form, and intention were all correct, the baptism would be valid, which means the sacrament actually takes place, but it would be illicit. Another example: a priest during Mass makes up his own offertory prayers, but says the correct words of consecration. Here the sacrament is valid—the bread and wine become the body and blood of Christ—but illicit, for he did not follow the liturgical laws regarding the Mass prayers.

A final requirement for sacraments to be valid is the proper intention. For the minister, this is somewhat vague: "The intention required is to will to do what the Church does" (CCC 1256). This is usually understood in a broad sense: the minister need not have full faith in the sacrament, as long as he has in mind to do what the Church does. For the person receiving the sacrament, again, the intention to receive it does not necessarily mean full faith, though that is certainly desirable. As long as they have the general intention to receive the sacrament, Catholics can receive the benefit of it. For example, practicing Catholics who only vaguely know about the sacrament of anointing of the sick, or who are unconscious due to illness or injury, can receive the sacramental grace if given that sacrament by a priest. Their faith carries with it the general intention to receive that sacrament when needed.

## 7. Why can only practicing Catholics receive the sacraments?

In establishing his covenant with the Israelites, God also established three different leadership roles: priests, prophets, and kings. The role of the Israelite priests was to offer sacrifices as God described to Moses and his brother Aaron; Aaron and his descendants were to be the priests. The prophets were God's spokesmen; he commissioned them to proclaim his laws and to warn the Israelites of the consequences when they violated these laws. Beginning with Saul, God appointed kings over the Israelites to govern them as a nation. Jesus fulfilled the Old Covenant by establishing a New Covenant, in which all three offices are present in himself. As priest, he offered the sacrifice of his body and blood on the cross, through which we receive his life, his grace. As prophet, he gave his teachings. As king, he claimed sovereignty over all nations of the world, mandating that all are obliged to recognize his reign.

These three roles are continued through the Catholic Church. Through the sacraments, by which Jesus gives his grace to mankind, the Church carries on the role of Christ as priest. But for the sacraments to have effect—to give grace—they must include the aspects of prophet and king, of moral teaching and of governance. In other words, for a sacrament to exist, it must *mean* something; this meaning is part of the teaching of Christ, preserved and explained by the Church. The sacrament of baptism, for example, not only gives grace but also involves the prophetic or teaching role of the Church, which teaches that the recipient of baptism is cleansed of original sin, becomes a temple of the Holy Spirit, and is received as a member of the Church. Furthermore, the ritual governs how the sacrament is practiced, specifying the matter (water) and the form (words) needed for baptism, as well as the ordinary minister (priest or deacon) of the sacrament. The grace of the sacrament, its meaning, and its practice require all three roles of the Church: priest, prophet, and king. The same is true of all the sacraments: all give grace, all convey teachings of Christ and his Church, and all are governed by the Church.

This is why those receiving the sacraments (apart from baptism, of course) must, to the best of their ability, be practicing Catholics, accepting the role of Christ and his Church as priest, prophet, and king. Denying these can prevent recipients from receiving the grace of the sacraments, and in some cases can even make a sacrament invalid. For example, Jesus said that in matrimony man and woman become one flesh, that no man could separate what God has joined, and that whoever divorces and remarries another commits adultery (Matt. 19:4–9). If a man or woman (or both) deny the teachings of Christ and the Church regarding the indissolubility of marriage—if they vow to love and honor each other for life but in reality do not believe that marriage is for life—the vows are invalid, the sacrament of matrimony does not take place, and the marriage may later be annulled (see answer 20).

Finally, those who knowingly and willingly do not practice the Faith, but still presume to receive the sacraments, commit the mortal sin of sacrilege: treating holy things with less than the respect they deserve. As St. Paul wrote in regard to receiving Holy Communion: "Whoever, therefore, eats the bread or drinks the cup of the Lord in an unworthy manner will be guilty of profaning the body and blood of the Lord. Let a man examine himself and so eat of the bread and drink of the cup. For anyone who eats and drinks without discerning the body eats and drinks judgment upon himself" (1 Cor. 11:27–29).

## 8. Why are there seven sacraments?

The ultimate answer to this question is that there are seven sacraments because that is the number Jesus instituted. But a deeper understanding of the sacraments can be gained if we think of their role in the spiritual life as analogous to aspects of natural life. "In order to exist," says the Catechism of the Council of Trent, "to preserve existence, and to contribute to his own and to the public good, seven things seem necessary to man: to be born, to grow, to be nurtured, to be cured when sick, when weak to be strengthened; as far as regards the public welfare: to have magistrates invested with the authority to govern, and to perpetuate himself and his species by legitimate offspring." Each of the sacraments corresponds to one of these seven needs.

People become Christians by being born again of water and the Holy Spirit (John 3:3–5). This life of the Spirit within Christians grows when they receive confirmation (Acts 1:8). They are nurtured by the Eucharist, which is Christ himself, the true bread come down from heaven. The cure to sickness is sacramental penance, which restores spiritual health after sins. To be strengthened when weak, both spiritually and physically, signifies the effects of the anointing of the sick. Holy orders is the sacrament by which Christ's mission as priest, prophet, and king is passed on through the apostles to all times and places in the Church. And by sacramentally establishing man and woman as one flesh, matrimony provides for new members of Christ's body, the Church.

Each sacrament is unique in that each is instituted by Christ to give a specific sacramental grace and is conferred by its own sacramental signs and ceremony. But we can also look at the sacraments by examining the relationship they have with one another. One group of sacraments, namely baptism, confirmation, and the Eucharist, are called the *sacraments of initiation*. They are the foundation of Christian life.[2] All members of the Church have the common vocation, or calling, to holiness and to increase the Church in the world; these three sacraments initiate members of the Church and give them the grace necessary to fulfill this common calling.

The sacraments of penance and anointing of the sick are called the *sacraments of healing.* While on our pilgrimage through this life, "We are still in our 'earthly tent,' subject to suffering, illness, and death" (CCC 1420). While living in this world with his own earthly body, Jesus healed the bodies and souls of many with whom he came in contact; he continues his healing of body and soul for Christians today in the sacraments of penance and anointing of the sick.

Holy orders and matrimony, which are called the *sacraments at the service of communion and mission,* give grace for their particular vocations that support the Body of Christ. In addition to sanctifying grace, these sacraments of service also provide graces needed to worthily fulfill the calling of service to the Church and the world: "These sacraments contribute in a special way to ecclesial communion and to the salvation of others" (*Compendium* 321).

Baptism, confirmation, and holy orders are different from the other sacraments in that these three imprint a permanent *character* or *seal* on the soul. That character "qualifies us to receive or perform something sacred, and distinguishes us by some mark" (Catechism of Trent). In baptism, the sacramental character qualifies those who receive it to receive the other sacraments, and it separates them from those who are not members of the Body of Christ. Confirmation also distinguishes those who have received it from those who have not—the latter are newborn infants in the Faith, rather than soldiers of Christ possessing the grace and the calling "to fight against our internal enemy and against the spiritual powers of wickedness in high places" (ibid.). Holy orders also has the twofold effect of distinguishing and commissioning: it makes men priests and enables them to act in the person of Christ in confecting the sacraments.

All three of these sacraments can be received only once; there would be no point in repeating them, because once given, the sacramental seal remains on the soul for all eternity. In contrast, anointing of the sick may be given any number of times, whenever Catholics become seriously infirm due to illness or old age. Matrimony may be repeated after one's spouse dies. Penance and Holy Communion may be received frequently, since forgiveness of sins and food for the soul are graces from which Catholics can benefit often.

## 9. What is the sacrament of baptism?

"Baptism is the sacrament of regeneration through water and in the word" (CCC 1213). The word itself means to *immerse*: in baptism, the immersion in water (or having it poured on the head) signifies "that all of us who have been baptized into Christ Jesus were baptized into his death. We were buried therefore with him by baptism into death, so that as Christ was raised from the dead by the glory of the Father, we too might walk in newness of life" (Rom. 6:3–4). Jesus underscored the importance of this sacrament when, just before his ascension into heaven, he said to his apostles, "Go therefore and make disciples of all nations, baptizing them in the name of the Father and of the Son and of the Holy Spirit, teaching them to observe all that I have commanded you" (Matt. 28:19–20). Baptism is the first sacrament to be received; without it, reception of the others is invalid and ineffectual:

> The Lord himself affirms that baptism is necessary for salvation. . . . The Church does not know of any means other than baptism that assures entry into eternal beatitude; this is why she takes care not to neglect the mission she has received from the Lord to see that all who can be baptized are "reborn of water and the Spirit" (John 3:5). God has bound salvation to the sacrament of baptism, but he himself is not bound by his sacraments (CCC 1257).

It's possible to receive the grace of baptism without the ordinary rite of the sacrament. Those who have not been baptized, but who are martyred for their faith in Christ, may still receive its effects: this is called *baptism by blood*. Similarly, those catechumens who are preparing for baptism but die before receiving it may also receive its effects in what is called *baptism of desire.* In fact anyone who is "ignorant of the gospel of Christ and of his Church, but seeks the truth and does the will of God in accordance with his understanding of it, [they] can be saved. It may be supposed that such persons would have desired baptism explicitly if they had known its necessity" (CCC 1260).

Jesus, of course, did not need baptism for himself, but to set an example he was baptized by John the Baptist in the Jordan River (Mark 1:9–11). John's baptism was not a sacrament; but by being baptized, Jesus emphasized the importance of the sacrament he would institute. The signs that Scripture describes accompanying the occasion manifested the effects the sacrament would bestow. Jesus' immersion in the water symbolizes the washing away of original sin; the voice of the Father identifying the Son represents those who are baptized becoming children by adoption; and the descent of the Holy Spirit upon him in the form of a dove shows that those who receive this sacrament become temples of the Holy Spirit, with his accompanying gifts and virtues.

The first effect of baptism is wiping away all sin and all punishment due to sin. Baptism is the only sacrament that takes away original sin, but it does not remove all of the effects of original sin. The human will is still inclined toward sin to some degree; this inclination, called *concupiscence*, is not a sin in itself. As a result of original sin, man's passions are also disordered; his intellect is clouded; and he suffers bodily weakness, sickness, and death. Baptism doesn't remove these effects of original sin connected to man's nature.

The first effect of baptism is to take away something—original sin—but its second effect is to *give* something: sanctifying grace. This grace is a share in the divine nature: the recipient becomes "a temple of the Holy Spirit" (CCC 1265). Closely related to this are the theological virtues (faith, hope, and charity), the moral virtues (prudence, justice, fortitude, and temperance), and the gifts of the Holy Spirit, all of which are given at baptism. Baptism also unites people to Christ and to his body, the Church. Finally, as Jesus' death on the cross opened the gates of heaven for all mankind, so the sacrament of baptism does so for those who are baptized: their true home is no longer on earth, but as adopted children of God and part of the mystical Body of Christ they are given the right to everlasting life in heaven.

The ordinary minister of baptism is a deacon or priest (this includes bishops). Under normal circumstances, baptism should be performed in a Church, by the proper minister, following the ritual of the Church. This includes using a baptism font, holy water, and the sacred oils blessed by the bishop. In cases of necessity, any person with the right intention may perform a baptism anywhere by pouring water on the person's head while saying *I baptize you in the name of the Father, and of the Son, and of the Holy Spirit* (CIC 861). If even a well-intentioned non-Christian has the thought of performing the Catholic ceremony with the effects that the Church believes, the baptism is valid. If this is done outside cases of necessity, the baptism is illicit but still valid.

Persons being baptized should have at least one sponsor, often called a *godparent*. The sponsor cannot be the person's parent, and must be a Catholic at least sixteen years of age who has received the sacraments of baptism, confirmation, and the Eucharist. In the 1917 *Code of Canon Law* (761), the person being baptized had to be given a Christian name: this was typically a saint's name, but may also have been something like Grace or Faith (or even Jesus, in some places). The current law merely says that "a name foreign to Christian sensibility is not given" (CIC 855). Presumably a priest would not baptize someone Lucifer, Mohammed, or Buddha; it is less clear if he should refuse to baptize using a name such as Squirrel, Kicker, or Puddin'head.

Jesus did not explicitly address the question as to whether infants should be baptized, but "It is not to be supposed that Christ the Lord would have withheld the sacrament and grace of baptism from children, of whom he said, 'Let the children come to me, and do not hinder them; for to such belongs the kingdom of heaven'" (Catechism of Trent; c.f. Matt. 19:14). The Bible describes two occasions on which St. Paul baptized entire families or households (Acts 16:33; 1 Corinthians 1:16), which would have included children below the age of reason. Although some Protestant groups today reject infant baptism, the practice is supported by Scripture and attested to in early Christian history.[3] Under normal circumstances, infants may be baptized as long as one or both parents (or legitimate guardian) request it, and there is a founded hope the child will be raised Catholic. But in danger of death, infants may be baptized even without the consent of either parent. These directives also apply to adults with the mental capacity of a child below the age of reason.

## 10. What is the sacrament of confirmation?

Jesus promised that he would give the Holy Spirit to the apostles (John 15:26–16:15). He fulfilled this promise on Easter Sunday, and more vividly on the feast of Pentecost (John 20:19–23, Acts 2:1–12). In the sacrament of confirmation, "The baptized are more perfectly bound to the Church and are enriched with a special strength of the Holy Spirit. Hence they are, as true witnesses of Christ, more strictly obliged to spread and defend the Faith by word and deed" (CCC 1285).

The name of the sacrament indicates its close connection with baptism; it is a *confirmation* of the indwelling of the Holy Spirit, and of the commission to spread the gospel, both of which are first given at baptism. Yet it is a distinct sacrament, as Scripture makes clear: "Now when the apostles at Jerusalem heard that

Samaria had received the word of God, they sent to them Peter and John, who came down and prayed for them that they might receive the Holy Spirit; for it had not yet fallen on any of them, but they had only been baptized in the name of the Lord Jesus" (Acts 8:14–16; cf. Acts 19:1–6).

The effects of confirmation are threefold: a sacramental character, an increase in sanctifying grace, and sacramental grace. In ancient times, soldiers received a seal identifying them with a particular leader; similarly, the sacramental seal of confirmation makes Christians *soldiers of Christ*, with the commission to live and spread the Faith, even amidst life-threatening danger. Each sacrament bestows a grace that has effects unique to it; the sacramental grace of confirmation enables Christians "to be stronger to resist all the assault of the world, the flesh, and the devil, while their minds are fully confirmed in faith to confess and glorify the name of our Lord Jesus Christ" (Catechism of Trent). Confirmation strengthens several other effects of baptism: "It roots us more deeply in the divine filiation, unites us more firmly to Christ, increases the gifts of the Holy Spirit in us, [and] renders our bond with the Church more perfect" (CCC 1303).

The ordinary minister of confirmation is the bishop, though he may delegate priests to give the sacrament. It is given by anointing with chrism, the perfumed oil blessed by the bishop at the Chrism Mass during

Holy Week. Confirmation is ordinarily given during Mass; the bishop (or priest) lays hands on the person, makes the sign of the cross on his forehead with the sacred chrism, and says, "Be sealed with the gift of the Holy Spirit." Although no one other than bishops and delegated priests can validly give confirmation, when someone is in danger of death a priest may do it without being delegated. Even infants should be confirmed if they are in such danger, for although they are not capable of using some of the gifts of confirmation, those gifts will be present for them in the future, if and when they are needed. Furthermore, if the infant dies, his soul will have been united more firmly to Christ, and be all the more glorious in heaven.

*Canon Law* specifies, "Every baptized person not yet confirmed . . . is capable of receiving confirmation" (CIC 889). Those receiving the sacrament should be instructed in the Faith, have the intention to receive the sacrament, and be capable of renewing their baptismal promises. But this renewal should not lead anyone to think that confirmation is simply a Catholic coming-of-age ceremony; it is a serious (and unfortunately common) error to say that confirmation is for those who were baptized as infants to "confirm" their faith in Christ. The proper age for receiving confirmation is after the age of reason (about age seven); bishops may determine the age at which the sacrament is ordinarily received in their dioceses. Eastern rite

Catholics routinely receive confirmation as infants, in the same ceremony as baptism, and they also receive the Eucharist at that time. All three sacraments are given by the priest.

As in baptism, those being confirmed should have sponsors whose role is to assist them in being faithful witnesses of Christ. In fact, it is a common practice for the baptism sponsor to be the confirmation sponsor, too. However, unlike baptism, which the Church considers valid in any Christian denomination that uses water and the trinitarian formula, confirmation in other denominations (other than the Eastern Orthodox churches) is invalid. Therefore, those coming into the Catholic Church from the Protestant denominations usually do not need to be baptized, but they do need to receive confirmation.

## 11. What is the sacrament of the Eucharist?

The different names for this sacrament help to explain its deep meaning. The word *Eucharist* comes from two Greek words meaning *good grace* or *thanksgiving*. Before eating a meal, many people "say grace": they offer a prayer of thanks for their meal. The Eucharist is Christ himself, the source of all good and all grace. In confecting the Eucharist, the Church gives thanks to God; when the members of the Church receive the Eucharist, they too give thanks.

This sacrament is also called *Holy Communion*, for those who worthily receive it are united with Christ, with his body the Church, and with one another. The Eucharist is the source of this union, since it is Jesus himself, and it also the sign of this union, since it is visible in itself and in the ritual that accompanies it.

The Eucharist is also called the *Blessed Sacrament* and the *Most Holy Sacrament of the Altar.* It is the only sacrament that persists in material form after it is given: in other words, whereas there is no change in the water at baptism and no change in the oil at confirmation, the bread and wine that become the body and blood of Christ remain so until they are consumed. It is the most blessed and most holy of the seven sacraments in the sense that it is Christ, and therefore the source of the grace that is given through all the sacraments. When received worthily, the Eucharist gives sanctifying grace as all do the sacraments, but it is the only sacrament whose purpose is to give this grace on a weekly or even daily basis. In addition, the Eucharist remits venial or lesser sins, provided the recipient is sorry for them and desires to be free of them. Related to this is the spiritual strength of the Eucharist to help resist the temptations to sin.

This sacrament is called the *Lord's Supper*, since Jesus gave it to his apostles at the Last Supper he ate with them before going to his passion and death. Furthermore, in the book of Revelation (19:9), an angel says, "Blessed are those who are invited to the marriage supper of the Lamb," indicating that the Eucharist is the supper of Jesus' marriage feast, his union with his bride, the Church. Jesus' actions at the Last Supper also give us the phrase *breaking of the bread* as a name for this sacrament: "With eyes raised to you, O God, his almighty Father, giving you thanks, he said the blessing, broke the bread" (Roman Canon).

The New Testament teaches clearly that: 1) Jesus promised to give his body and blood as food for his disciples; 2) he indeed gave them this sacrament and commissioned them to perpetuate it; and 3) his disciples passed it on through the Church.

After the miraculous multiplication of loaves of bread to feed the multitude, Jesus told them that he would give his body as food:

"I am the living bread which came down from heaven; if any one eats of this bread, he will live forever; and the bread which I shall give for the life of the world is my flesh." The Jews then disputed among themselves, saying, "How can this man give us his flesh to eat?" So Jesus said to them, "Truly, truly, I say to you, unless you eat the flesh of the Son of man and drink his blood, you have no life in you; he who eats my flesh and drinks my blood has eternal life, and I will raise him up at the last day. For my flesh is food indeed, and my blood is drink indeed" (John 6:51–54).

Seeing how clear and adamant Jesus was in teaching that the Eucharist is truly his body, it makes no sense to believe that this sacrament is merely a *symbol* of his body. Indeed, the crowd understood what he was saying, and had a hard time swallowing it: "Many of his disciples, when they heard it, said, 'This is a hard saying; who can listen to it?' After this many of his disciples drew back and no longer went about with him" (John 6:60, 66). Believing that bread is a symbol of his flesh would not be a "hard saying," but believing that the bread actually becomes his flesh is difficult; it requires faith.

The night before he died, Jesus kept his promise, changing bread and wine into his body and blood and giving it to his disciples to eat and drink. He also stated unequivocally that they were to do the same: "And he took bread, and when he had given thanks he broke it and gave it to them, saying, 'This is my body which is given for you. Do this in remembrance of me'" (Luke 22:19). St. Paul reminded the people of Corinth that in giving them the Eucharist, he was following the command to celebrate the sacrament of Jesus' body and blood:

> For I received from the Lord what I also delivered to you, that the Lord Jesus on the night when he was betrayed took bread, and when he had given thanks, he broke it, and said, "This is my body which is for

you. Do this in remembrance of me." In the same way also the cup, after supper, saying, "This cup is the New Covenant in my blood. Do this, as often as you drink it, in remembrance of me." For as often as you eat this bread and drink the cup, you proclaim the Lord's death until he comes (1 Cor. 11:23–26).

Paul reinforced Jesus' teaching that the Eucharist is given to the Church not just at the Last Supper but *until he comes*—until the end of the world.

## 12. What is the Mass?

The Mass and the Eucharist are part of the same sacramental mystery, but the meaning of the two words is not identical: the Eucharist is the *sacrament*, and the Mass is the *sacrifice*. A person consumes the Eucharist, and the Eucharist can be kept in a tabernacle; but it would be incorrect to say that a person consumes the Mass, or that the Mass is kept in a tabernacle. Another name for the Mass is the *Eucharistic liturgy*, or ritual in which the Eucharist is offered and received.

The word *Mass* comes from the Latin, *Ite Missa est*, ("Go, you are sent,") the words the priest says at the end of the traditional Latin Rite. As baptism makes us temples of the Holy Spirit and members of the Church, and confirmation gives us the grace and gifts of the Holy Spirit to be soldiers of Christ, we come to Mass to receive the body of Christ to renew this strength and are sent forth to live the Faith.

The Mass may be divided into two parts: the *Liturgy of the Word* and the *Liturgy of the Eucharist*. Traditionally called the *Mass of the Catechumens* and the *Mass of the Faithful*, in former times those who were not yet baptized—the catechumens—would depart after the readings and homily; only the baptized were present for the remainder of the liturgy. The Liturgy of the Eucharist primarily consists of the three parts necessary for the sacrifice to take place. First is the offertory, where the bread and wine (in which a little water is added) are offered to God. The bread and wine may be brought forward in procession, along with "money or other gifts for the poor or for the Church, brought by the faithful or collected in the church; they are to be put in a suitable place away from the eucharistic table."[4]

Following the offertory is the Canon or Eucharistic Prayer, which is the heart of the Mass. When the priest says the words of consecration—*This is my body . . . This is the chalice of my blood*—the bread and wine on the altar become the body and blood of Christ. This change is called *transubstantiation*, which indicates that the substance has changed: there is no longer bread and wine on the altar, only Christ. As we noted, the appearances of bread and wine remain: the human senses cannot detect any difference, and any scientific tests performed would find only bread and wine.

It is purely an act of faith in Christ and his Church to believe that by a miracle, the risen Christ who is present in heaven also becomes present on the altar.

Not only his body and blood, but also Christ's human soul and his divine nature are present in the Eucharist. Although there is a sacramental separation in which the bread and wine are consecrated using different words, the whole Christ is fully present in each *species* of the Eucharist: in every particle of the host and in every drop in the chalice. (That's why there is no strict need for anyone other than the priest to drink from the chalice, since everyone who receives the host receives the whole Christ.)

The final part of the sacrifice is the priest's communion: for a sacrifice to take place, the object being sacrificed must be destroyed or consumed. The Israelites did both, depending on the sacrifice: they might have burned the animal that had been sacrificed, they might have eaten it, or they might have eaten part and burned part. At Mass, the sacrifice is consummated—completed—when the priest consumes Christ's body and blood. The Communion of the faithful, while of priceless value for their souls, is not essential to the Mass being offered. In fact, although they should have someone present if possible, priests can offer Mass alone if need be: "Daily celebration is recommended earnestly since, even if the faithful cannot be present, it is the act of Christ and the Church in which priests fulfill their principal function" (CIC 904).

Recall that a valid sacrament is one that has the necessary matter, form, minister, and intention. Without these, the ceremony is invalid, and the sacrament does not actually take place. For the consecration of the Eucharist to be valid, that is, for the bread and wine to become the body and blood of Christ, "The bread must be wheaten only, and recently made, so that there is no danger of corruption. The wine must be natural, made from grapes of the vine, and not corrupt" (CIC 924). It should go without saying that only an ordained priest has the ability to validly offer Mass; provided he has the intention to do what the Church does and uses the proper bread and wine, the sacrament is valid.

It is also important that the priest offer the Mass licitly—that he follows the laws of the Church. The people have the right to the Mass being offered as directed in the liturgical books of the Church: "The priest will remember that he is the servant of the sacred liturgy and that he himself is not permitted, on his own initiative, to add, to remove, or to change anything in the celebration of Mass."[5] If the priest makes changes not given in the liturgical books, such as having a hand puppet preach the homily or dressing as Barney the dinosaur while giving the blessing, these parts are not licit.

## 13. What are the spiritual benefits of the Mass?

Some 2,000 years ago, outside the city of Jerusalem,

Jesus offered his life as a sacrifice for the sins of all. It was a unique sacrifice in that he offered himself: he was both the priest and the victim. The Last Supper was the same sacrifice, since he was offering himself there as well; the difference was the time, the place, the appearance of his body and blood, and the fact that he did not die at the Last Supper—it was an *unbloody* sacrifice. Every Mass is also the same sacrifice as the cross, in that Jesus is always the priest and the victim. As was the Last Supper, the Mass is an unbloody sacrifice: it differs in time, place, and appearance from the Cross.

Mass has been offered since the time of Christ to the present day, and it has been offered on altars all over the world. Priests act *in persona Christi*, in the person of Christ; they are truly offering the sacrifice of Christ's body and blood, but only by the power of Christ, who is the eternal High Priest. This sacrifice bears abundant and varied fruit, according to who is benefitted: "The *general* fruit which benefits all the faithful, living and dead; a *special* fruit received by the faithful who assist at Mass; the *personal* fruit received by the priest offering the sacrifice; the *ministerial* fruit which benefits those for whom the Mass is offered."[6] The *value* of the Mass is said to be infinite, because Jesus, both as priest and as victim, is perfect; the sacrifice of the Mass, like that of the cross, is the perfect sacrifice. Although it is both infinite and perfect due to Christ being infinite (as God) and perfect (as God and man), the effects of the Mass are limited, due to the imperfection of human beings receiving the effects. As with all religious sacrifice (and prayer), there are five potential *effects* of the Mass: worship (or adoration), thanksgiving, impetration (asking for grace), forgiveness of sins, and satisfaction for the punishment due to sins.

Mass is the perfect act of worship in that it is Christ's act of worship. It is imperfect in the sense that the human worshippers are not perfect, both in the state of their souls and in their mental and physical acts of worship. Regarding the latter, the faithful can take steps to worship to the best of their ability, including looking at the readings in advance, arriving at church before Mass begins in order to prepare and staying after it ends to give thanks, developing a habit of ignoring distractions, and even wearing formal attire. Obviously these are not possible for all people all of the time, as any mother with children will be quick to point out. The point is for those attending Mass to give the best worship they can; for busy mothers (and fathers) of young children, getting them to Mass and home again in one piece can be a prodigious act of worship.

Mass is also the perfect act of thanksgiving. Giving a gift is a way to give thanks; the gift of God the Son, Jesus Christ, to God the Father is the perfect gift and therefore the perfect act of thanksgiving. Though the reasons for giving thanks to God are countless, they can be summarized in just three: creation, redemption, and sanctification (CCC 1328). We can thank God for creating us in his image and giving us an immortal soul; we can thank him for the other human beings he has created, all of whom he desires to spend eternity with him in heaven; we can thank him for the creation of his angels and sending them as guardians; we can thank him for the rest of the universe, both the living and inanimate creatures (Dan. 3:51–90). Of course the greatest gift for which man gives thanks to God is the gift of the Son, Jesus Christ.

Mass is the perfect prayer of impetration, or asking God for grace. The Mass itself gives grace not only to those who are present, but for the entire Church: "Accept and bless these gifts, these offerings, these holy and unblemished sacrifices," reads the first Eucharistic Prayer, "which we offer you firstly for your holy Catholic Church."

The last two effects of the Mass, though distinct, are closely related, and may be considered together. Because it is the same sacrifice of Christ on the cross, the Mass grants forgiveness of sins and satisfaction for the punishment due to sins. As with the other effects, these are infinite at their source but finite in their reception. The limitations come from sinful humanity: failing to be sorry for sins is an obstacle to being forgiven; and the punishment cannot be fully remitted unless we resolve, with the help of God's grace, to do penance, amend our lives, and avoid the near occasions of sin.

## 14. What is the sacrament of penance?

Penance is the sacrament in which Christians, after baptism, "obtain pardon from God's mercy for the offense committed against him, and are, at the same time, reconciled with the Church which they have wounded by their sins and which by charity, by example, and by prayer labors for their conversion" (CCC 1422).

The word *penance* may be defined as heartfelt sorrow for sins, and outward expression of this sorrow, because they offend God. The sacrament of penance lifts this sorrow to a higher level: "It consecrates the Christian sinner's personal and ecclesial steps of conversion, penance, and satisfaction" (CCC 1423). This sacrament is also called *confession*, a word which has several meanings: it is the acknowledgement of sins and offenses, but it also means the acknowledgment of faith and open praise of God, the object of faith. The sacrament of penance includes both these aspects (CCC 1424). It is also called *reconciliation*, since it reconciles, or restores peace and friendship, between the sinner and God and the Church.

To be a disciple of Christ includes repentance of sins, professing faith in Jesus Christ as Savior, accepting his teachings, and being baptized in the name of the Father, Son, and Holy Spirit (cf. Matt. 28:18–20; Mark 1:15; John 3:5). But this initial conversion is not enough: after repenting of sins and being baptized, Christians still have the inclination to sin (Rom. 7:18–19), also called *concupiscence,* and this leads to the commission of more sins during life.

Immediately following his resurrection, Jesus instituted the sacrament of penance as the ordinary means of forgiving the sins of Christians when he gave to the apostles his authority to forgive: "'As the Father has sent me, even so I send you.' And when he had said this, he breathed on them and said to them, 'Receive the Holy Spirit. If you forgive the sins of any, they are forgiven; if you retain the sins of any, they are retained'" (John 20:21–23). These verses describe the sacrament in detail. As the Father sent Jesus to forgive men's sins, so he sends the apostles to continue this work—not by their own power but by the power of the Holy Spirit. Amazingly, they also are given the authority to retain sins, too—for example, when someone expresses no sorrow or purpose of amending his life. That power has passed from Christ to the apostles to their successors in the Church to this day.

Some Christians doubt the need for this sacrament, claiming that that there is no need for forgiveness of sins after people have accepted Christ, since his death paid for those sins once and for all. This clearly contradicts the teachings of Jesus and the apostles (see Matt. 7:21–23; 1 Cor. 4:3–5; 1 John 1:8–10; Rev. 2:1–3:22). The process of conversion is not an individual effort but is the result of God's grace and the mission that Christ entrusted to his Church: "Christ's call to conversion continues to resound in the lives of Christians. This second conversion is an uninterrupted task for the whole Church. This endeavor of conversion is not just a human work. It is the movement of a 'contrite heart,' drawn and moved by grace to respond to the merciful love of God who loved us first" (CCC 1428).

When we have committed mortal sin, the most important effect of the sacrament of penance is the forgiveness of sins. Before the sacrament, we are bereft of divine life, are no longer children of God, and have the gates of heaven closed to us; upon receiving the sacrament, our soul is brought back to life, we are restored to divine sonship and the life of the Church, and we regain our place in heaven.

The sacrament has other effects, even for those who have not committed such serious sins. Venial sins are (of course) also forgiven. Sanctifying grace is restored if it was lost through serious sin and is strengthened if it was already present. As an integral part of the sacrament, penance "[is] performed by the penitent in order to repair the harm caused by sin and to re-establish habits befitting a disciple of Christ" (CCC 1494). Finally, at least some measure of Christian joy and peace of mind accompany the state of grace that the soul experiences with receiving this sacrament.

## 15. How is the sacrament of penance performed?

The following are the steps in making a good confession:

- We do a careful examination of conscience, honestly evaluating ourselves for sins we have committed and good we failed to do.

- We confess all serious sin in kind and number, along with other sins we wish to name.

- We express sincere sorrow for our sins, and state our intention to amend our life.

- The priest gives advice and encouragement to help us in these resolutions.

- He gives us a penance to perform and says the words of absolution.

- We perform the penance.

Only priests can validly absolve sins in the sacrament of penance; there is no extraordinary minister of this sacrament. Priests must also have the *faculty* to exercise the power to absolve sins. This is a somewhat complex legal term; essentially it is the Church safeguarding the sacrament and preventing abuses. For example, if a priest is involved in a serious scandal, his bishop (or superior, if he is in a religious order) has the authority to revoke the priest's faculties, thereby preventing him from performing the sacrament (CIC 966). But if persons going to confession mistakenly think that priest has the faculty to absolve their sins, then the sins are nonetheless forgiven (CIC 144). And if a person is in danger of death, then a priest whose faculties have been revoked, or even a priest who has left the active priesthood, can and should perform the sacrament for the dying person.

Priests are forbidden to reveal what they hear from penitents (CIC 983); this is commonly called the *seal of confession*. If priests hear someone confess a horrible crime such as murder or child abuse they can encourage the penitent to turn himself in to legal authorities (though they cannot make that a condition for absolution) but may not make known to anyone what was confessed. In fact, even if there is no danger of their sins being disclosed, the priest may not use the knowledge from confessions in any way that is detrimental to the penitents (CIC 984). For example, suppose a woman confessed that she was stealing from her workplace. The priest could not then attempt to help the employer by advising him to fire the employee for some other reason.

The seal of confession forbids the priest to reveal penitents' sins in any way, to any degree. When the confession has ended, the priest should never mention anything about it, even to that penitent himself. While it may not technically be a violation of the seal of confession to speak later to penitents about their own confession, it is still a violation of the secrecy they have a right to expect. A priest should never tell stories about something he heard in confession, for any reason, no matter how long ago or far away the confession took place; nor should he ever acknowledge to anyone whether or not another individual went to confession. If a priest wants to ask another priest for advice about a difficult matter he heard in confession, he should change some of the circumstantial details.

The priest should explain to penitents the nature of their confession, or the sacrament in general, as needed. For example, if they confess missing Mass because of health problems that prevent them from attending, the priest should tell them that is not a sin; if they were to express concern about their sins being revealed, the priest should explain to them the inviolability of the seal of confession. Similarly, penitents who are unsure about whether to confess something should ask the priest about their concern. The priest may then ask questions of the penitent and counsel him in properly examining his conscience.

The form of this sacrament is the words of absolution spoken aloud by the priest:

> God the Father of mercies, through the death and resurrection of his son, has reconciled the world to himself, and sent the Holy Spirit among us for the forgiveness of sins. Through the ministry of the

Church, may God give you pardon and peace, and I absolve you from your sins, in the name of the Father, and of the Son, and of the Holy Spirit.

In case of necessity, the words of absolution may be shortened to "I absolve you from your sins, in the name of the Father, and of the Son, and of the Holy Spirit."

The matter for most of the sacraments is something physical, such as water for baptism, oil for confirmation, and bread and wine for the Eucharist. Penance is different in that there is no such substance involved. The *remote matter* is the penitents' sins: just as wood that is consumed by flames is the matter for a fire, so the sins that are consumed are the matter for this sacrament. They are remote in the sense that they are not taking place during the confession. The *proximate* matter is the acts the penitents perform as part of the sacrament, specifically contrition, confession, and satisfaction or penance. For sins to be absolved and the grace of the sacrament to be received, penitents must confess, in kind and in number, all serious sins (of which they are aware) committed since baptism that have not been previously confessed.

This is made clear by keeping in mind what is happening in the sacrament: those with mortal sins have broken their relationship with God and desire to be reconciled with him. In order to restore the broken relationship they must truly be sorry and express their sorrow or contrition for every serious sin; deliberately holding back a serious sin prevents the absolution from being effective, and that sin remains an obstacle preventing the restoring of the relationship with Christ.

When we go to confession we may, but do not have to, name some or all of our venial (lesser) sins, as well. Mentally and emotionally, it can be very helpful to name those sins that we are most reluctant to confess: it can be a great relief to state them aloud, and to hear a human voice say in response, *I absolve you . . . Go in peace*. We must also have a firm purpose of amending our lives, which includes doing the penance that the priest indicates and having the intention of avoiding *near occasions* of sin—situations that we know can tempt us to sin.

The penance from which this sacrament takes its name is the prayer or good work or act of self-denial that the priest gives the person to perform. Jesus paid the price for our sins through his suffering and death, but he also told his disciples, "If any man would come after me, let him deny himself and take up his cross and follow me" (Matt. 16:24). The penance we do as part of this sacrament is united to the suffering of Christ: "Such penances help configure us to Christ, who alone expiated our sins once for all" (CCC 1460). As a comparison, suppose that by disobedience to his parents a child breaks a window. The parents pay the price for it, because the child is unable. Out of justice, the parents make the child contribute what he can. We are unable to pay for our sins; out of love for us, Jesus paid the price, but out of justice, he also requires us to do penance for them.

Under very narrow circumstances, the Church allows a priest to give absolution to many people at once, without their first having confessed their sins. This is called *general absolution*, and is only done in an emergency where there is a large number of people in immediate need of the sacrament, such as a brigade of soldiers going into battle or passengers on an aircraft in danger of crashing. In such cases, the priest tells the penitents that they must still go to individual confession when the emergency is over (CIC 960–961). Under no circumstances may a priest tell penitents that they only need to name one sin; neither may a priest listen to multiple confessions, then give one absolution to all the penitents. These time-saving tricks are not part of validly absolving sins.

### 16. What is the sacrament of anointing of the sick?

"The anointing of the sick [is the sacrament] by which the Church commends to the suffering and glorified Lord the faithful who are dangerously ill so that he may support and save them" (CIC 998). This sacrament was formerly called *extreme unction*, indicating that it is an unction, or anointing, given in serious cases of illness or injury. The Gospels show that Jesus insinuated this sacrament: "And he called to him the Twelve, and began to send them out two by two, and gave them authority over the unclean spirits . . . And they cast out many demons, and anointed with oil many that were sick and healed them" (Mark 6:7, 13). In his New Testament letter, St. James promulgated the sacrament for the Church: "Is any among you sick? Let him call for the elders of the Church, and let them pray over him, anointing him with oil in the name of the Lord; and the prayer of faith will save the sick man, and the Lord will raise him up; and if he has committed sins, he will be forgiven" (James 5:14–15).

Anointing of the sick gives sanctifying grace to those who receive it worthily, and it gives its own unique sacramental grace, which has several effects. As anointing with oil is a means of showing that God is commissioning someone to a particular calling and giving the grace to fulfill it, this sacrament consecrates the suffering of the sick, "uniting of the sick person to the passion of Christ, for his own good and that of the whole Church" (CCC 1532). It also gives strength, peace, and courage to bear difficulties that accompany serious illness or injury, or the frailty of old age. This includes renewed trust in God and strength to resist the temptations of the devil and the flesh that may come. The sacrament also "completes our conformity to the death and resurrection of Christ, just as baptism began it. This last anointing fortifies the end of our earthly life" (CCC 1523).

Another effect of this sacrament is the forgiveness of sins and some degree of healing the spiritual sloth that results from sin. This forgiveness primarily refers to venial sins: recipients should go to confession first if possible, but if they cannot, even mortal sins are forgiven for those who are habitually sorry for them (*Compendium* 319). The remission of the punishment due to sin is always dependent upon the degree to which individuals remain attached to their sins. The last effect of anointing of the sick is the restoration of physical health, if it is at the same time beneficial to the salvation of the soul. As hard as it is for those who are grieving the death of their loved one, God knows when it is best for each soul to depart from this life.

Only a priest can validly give the anointing of the sick; the sacrament does not take place if the ritual is performed by anyone else. Priests typically give the sacrament to those committed to their care, i.e. parish priests to their parishioners, school chaplains to students, hospital chaplains to their patients, and military chaplains to those in the armed forces. But any priest can give the sacrament to any member of the faithful, even to someone not directly in his care; as a practical matter he should inform the proper priest that he has done so. Similarly, any Catholics who believe they have a serious health problem can and should contact a priest in order to receive this sacrament.

"The anointing of the sick can be administered to no member of the faithful who, having reached the use of reason, begins to be in danger by reason of illness or old age. If there is any doubt as to whether the sick person has reached the use of reason, or is dangerously ill, or is dead, this sacrament is to be administered" (CIC 1004–1005). There is no limit to the number of times people may receive this sacrament: if they recover and then become sick again, they may receive it again; if they receive it and later their condition worsens, they may receive it again. However, anointing of the sick is not to be given to healthy individuals in danger of death, such as soldiers going to war or passengers on a sinking ship, since they are not sick; general absolution may be given in such extreme circumstances. Neither should it be given to those slightly ill, or those feeling merely distraught.

Many people assume that anointing of the sick is given to those only in immediate danger of death. However, the Church has always instructed the priest *not* to wait until death is inevitable to give the sacrament: "This sacrament restores health of body (should it be for the good of the soul) by assisting the powers of nature; and hence it should not be deferred until recovery is despaired of."[7] A person may still be anointed if his breathing and heartbeat have stopped, since he might yet be revived; furthermore, it is not known precisely when the soul leaves the body.

Although Jesus raised several dead people to life, and on at least one occasion healed someone who was at the point of death, most of his miraculous cures involved those who had serious conditions but were not dying. He restored the senses of the deaf, mute, and blind; he gave paralytics and the crippled the power to walk; he cured leprosy and other diseases. In anointing of the sick, the Church sees Jesus' work as a model, praying for miraculous cures of those at the point of death, but not waiting until that point to give the sacrament to those suffering from serious health conditions. For example, priests typically anoint people before major surgery, people diagnosed with cancer, even if the prognosis is good, people whose condition requires more than just a day-long hospital stay, and those being treated in the hospital intensive care unit.

Children who have reached the age of reason may receive the sacrament (CIC 1004). (Baptized Christians who have not reached that point are in a perfect state of grace and so do not need to be anointed.) The only Catholics who may not receive this sacrament are those who obstinately persist in a manifestly grave sin (CIC 1007). Persistence in grave sin indicates a spiritual disposition that is not compatible with the sacrament. Persons in such a state should first reconcile with God through the sacrament of penance.

## 17. What is the sacrament of holy orders?

"Holy orders is the sacrament through which the mission entrusted by Christ to his apostles continues to be exercised in the Church until the end of time: thus it is the sacrament of apostolic ministry. It includes three degrees: episcopate [bishop], presbyterate [priest], and diaconate [deacon]" (CCC 1536). The Latin world *ordo* means an order, rank, or line, as in an organization or unit of soldiers. Like baptism and confirmation, this sacrament imprints a permanent seal or character on the soul of the man receiving it, establishing him for all eternity in the particular order, which in itself is a holy institution. The sacrament is conferred by the bishop laying his hands on the man to be ordained, and saying the prayer according to the rite for the particular order; these constitute the matter and form. In addition to giving sanctifying grace, holy orders bestows sacramental grace to empower the ordained to worthily carry out their office.

In recent decades there have been Catholics and non-Catholics promoting the ordination of women to the priesthood. (Women have never been given the sacrament of holy orders, neither by Jesus nor by his apostles; by the Latin or Eastern churches; in ancient, medieval, or modern times.) Some say that Jesus would have ordained women, but was constrained by attitudes of his time and culture. This is a weak argument, since we know that Jesus broke from so many conventions of his day, especially those of the ruling Israelite class, that he was put to death. Why would he have been a conformist in this once instance? Furthermore, we see Jesus elsewhere breaking custom and elevating the status of women: allowing the woman with a hemorrhage to touch him, speaking with the Samaritan woman, and entrusting Mary Magdalene to be the first to share the news of his resurrection.

Scripture shows Jesus calling only men to the priesthood, and early Christian history shows only men serving as priests. This was not because men were holier; the Blessed Virgin Mary holds a higher place in the Church and in heaven than the apostles, yet Jesus did not call her to the priesthood. If the priesthood was to be based on sanctity, Jesus' mother would have been the very first choice. But his choice only of men for the priesthood shows that biological sex is an intrinsic part of the matter of this sacrament, in which the priest mysteriously becomes an *alter Christus* (another Christ) before the altar.[8]

God established a type of orders in the Old Testament, setting apart from the rest of Israel the tribe of Levi to perform religious duties (Num. 18:2–6). Later, as he freed the Israelites from slavery in Egypt and gave them the promised land, God directed that Moses' brother Aaron and his descendants should be priests, commissioned to enter the holy of holies and offer sacrifices (Exod. 28:1 ff). The priesthood of that order was passed on by lineage, the tribe, and family to which the priests belonged.

But the first priest named in the Bible was not of that line: "And Melchizedek King of Salem brought out bread and wine; he was priest of God Most High. And he blessed him and said, "Blessed be Abram by God Most High, maker of heaven and earth; and blessed be God Most High, who has delivered your enemies into your hand" (Gen. 14:18–20). The book of Psalms foretold that the Savior would be also be a priest:

> The Lord says to my lord: "Sit at my right hand, till I make your enemies your footstool." The Lord sends forth from Zion your mighty scepter. Rule in the midst of your foes! Your people will offer themselves freely on the day you lead your host upon the holy mountains. From the womb of the morning like dew your youth will come to you. The Lord has sworn and will not change his mind, "You are a priest forever after the order of Melchizedek" (Ps. 110:1–4; cf. Heb. 7:1–17).

Jesus was not of the tribe of Levi, nor was he a descendant of Aaron; rather, he fulfilled the prophecy of the priesthood of Melchizedek. He changed the bread and wine into his own body and blood at the Last Supper, and at the same time he instituted the Catholic priesthood by commissioning the apostles to continue the sacrifice: "Do this in remembrance of me" (Luke 22:19). Having already given them the power to offer the Mass, on Easter Sunday Jesus granted the apostles the power to forgive and retain sins, thereby completing the establishment of the priesthood in its fullness. As we have seen, priests are the ministers of anointing of the sick, and—if delegated by their bishop—they have power to confer the sacrament of confirmation.

The order of bishop is a higher level of orders, one that was held by the apostles and passed on by them (Acts 1:8, 21–26; 1 Tim. 3:1–7). Only bishops have the power to confer the sacrament of holy orders. This is related to the doctrine of *apostolic succession*, which means that the sacraments, especially those requiring the ministry of priests, are dependent upon the true and valid ordination of priests and consecration of bishops, who themselves were ordained and consecrated by bishops before them: "The fullness of the means of salvation which he [Christ] has willed: correct and complete confession of faith, full sacramental life, and ordained ministry in apostolic succession. The Church was, in this fundamental sense, Catholic on the day of Pentecost and will always be so until the day of the Parousia" (CCC 830). A bishop requires a mandate from the pope to consecrate anyone as bishop; without such a mandate, the consecration is still valid but illicit.

The word *deacon* comes from the Greek *diakonos* meaning *servant*. The order of deacons was established by the apostles in order to assist them in their ministry of serving the Church (Acts 1:1–6; 1 Tim. 3:8–13). Along with priests and bishops, deacons are ordinary ministers of Holy Communion: they may always distribute the Eucharist at Mass, even if a priest is present and is not doing so. Deacons are also ordinary ministers of baptism and may preside over the sacrament of matrimony.

At least some of the apostles (all priests) were married, and many Eastern Catholic churches have their own tradition of allowing married men to be ordained (though their bishops are celibate). In the West (the Latin Rite, to which most Catholics belong), following the example of Jesus and the teaching of St. Paul, priests and bishops have, as a rule, been celibate since the early centuries of the Church. There have been exceptions to the rule, however. Mandatory celibacy for priests and bishops is not a matter of doctrine, but of practice, and the Church may modify or grant exceptions to it. This is in distinction to the ordination of women, which the Church—including the pope—has no authority to do; such ordinations would be invalid (CIC 1024).

Although deacons, priests, and bishops have in their souls the permanent character of holy orders, they can be *laicized,* or returned to the lay state according to the law of the Church. Laicized priests and bishops are no longer considered clergy, but they still have the inherent ability to perform sacraments. Though they can never licitly offer Mass, in cases when Catholics are in danger of death they may provide the sacraments of confirmation, penance, and anointing of the sick (CIC 883.3, 986.2, 1003).

## 18. What is the sacrament of matrimony?

"The matrimonial covenant, by which a man and a woman establish between themselves a partnership of the whole of life, is by its nature ordered toward the good of the spouses and the procreation and education of offspring; this covenant between baptized persons has been raised by Christ the Lord to the dignity of a sacrament" (CCC 1601). There are any number of ways of looking at the effects, ends, blessings, goods, purposes, and properties of matrimony—perhaps the simplest is to look at each part of the definition.

The gift of God's grace is one effect of matrimony. Because matrimony is "this covenant between baptized persons [that] has been raised by Christ the Lord to the dignity of a sacrament," it gives grace, divine life, to those who receive it. In addition to the sanctifying grace given by all sacraments, matrimony gives sacramental grace, which is God's life assisting the married couple in fulfilling their vocations as husband and wife, and also as parents if God gives them children.

The second effect of matrimony is the sacramental bond, the partnership between husband and wife. This bond has two properties. The first is *unity*; as Jesus said, "So they are no longer two, but one flesh" (Matt. 19:6; cf. Gen. 2:24). There cannot be two men, two women, one man with more than one woman, one woman with more than one man, or any other combination. The second property is *indissolubility*: the partnership endures for life—until the death of one of the spouses; the surviving spouse is then able to marry again.

Jesus was very clear on the indissolubility of marriage: "What therefore God has joined together, let not man put asunder. For your hardness of heart Moses allowed you to divorce your wives, but from the beginning it was not so. And I say to you: whoever divorces his wife, except for unchastity, and marries another, commits adultery" (Matt. 19:6, 8–9). In this way Jesus raised marriage to the level of a sacrament; there would have been no reason to do so if he had wanted to allow divorce and remarriage. The indissolubility of marriage is a challenging teaching—even for the apostles, some of whom replied, "If such is the case of a man with his wife, it is not expedient to marry" (Matt. 19:10). Yet the teaching is rooted in the inseparability between Christ and his Church (Eph. 5:32). Jesus' marriage to his bride, the Church, is the model for Christian marriage: both are based on unconditional love, are established by God, and cannot be separated by man. Though it certainly can be difficult, even on a purely human level the permanence of marriage is a gift, not a punishment.

When a man and woman desire to pledge their love for one another for the rest of their lives, Jesus gives them a sacrament to help them fulfill this desire.

Matrimony is also said to have two ends or purposes: "the good of the spouses and the procreation and education of offspring" (CCC 1601). The good of the spouses includes love and fidelity, as stated in the marriage vows: "I promise to be true to you in good times and in bad, in sickness and in health. I will love you and honor you all the days of my life." *Procreation and education of children* is the other end of marriage. Of course not all married couples are capable of conceiving children; they are a gift from God. But sexual relations, appropriately called the *marriage act*, are by nature ordered toward the creation of new human life: "And God blessed them, and God said to them, 'Be fruitful and multiply, and fill the earth and subdue it'" (Gen. 1:28). Because the end or purpose of every human life is to spend eternity in heaven with God, educating children in the teachings of Christ is inherently part of the end or purpose of marriage.

In regard to matter and form, the other sacraments (except penance) have some physical sign that constitutes the matter, such as water, oil, or bread and wine. In matrimony, traditionally it is said that the man and woman *themselves* constitute remote matter, in that they give their bodies to one another: "[Jesus said] But from the beginning of creation, 'God made them male and female. For this reason a man shall leave his father and mother and be joined to his wife, and the two shall become one flesh.' So they are no longer two but one flesh. What therefore God has joined together, let not man put asunder" (Mark 10:6–9; cf. Gen. 2:24). The *proximate* matter is said to be the man and woman expressing this self-giving; similarly, the form of the sacrament is the acceptance of that consent.

A simpler view is that the vows constitute both the matter and form of the sacrament (CCC 1626–27). The man and woman themselves are the ministers of the sacrament; the priest or deacon who ordinarily presides over the rite is not the minister but rather receives the consent of the couple in the name of the Church and gives them the blessing of the Church (CCC 1623, 1630). If there are circumstances in which no priest or deacon is available for some length of time, the couple may validly marry; this should be done according to the Church ritual and in the presence of witnesses (CIC 1112–1116).

## 19. What is an annulment?

As we have seen, marriage is for life: when a man and woman are joined in the sacrament of matrimony,[9] the two become one flesh, and no man may separate what God has joined (see also Mark 10:6–9). To separate from someone to whom you have been validly married and go to live with someone else as husband and wife, even after a civil divorce and another wedding ceremony in city hall or a church, is to commit adultery.

Sometimes, however, a Catholic may attempt a valid marital union, but none takes place. There is a ceremony and an exchange of vows, but no sacrament and no marriage. When requested by one or both spouses, usually because they wish to marry another, a special Church court called a *tribunal* undertakes a rigorous investigation to determine whether the marriage was in fact never validly contracted (always beginning with the presumption that it was); this finding is called an *annulment*.

Often, marriages are found to be invalid and annulments granted on the basis of some defect in the exchange of vows that is part of the sacrament's form. In the marriage ceremony, just before the exchange of vows, the couple answers three questions:

- Have you come here freely and without reservation to give yourselves to each other in marriage?

- Will you love and honor each other as man and wife for the rest of your lives?

- Will you accept children willingly from God, and bring them up according to the law of Christ and his Church?

In order for the marriage to take place, the couple must answer affirmatively to these questions. If one or both individuals are found to have been incapable of consent or to have made statements contrary to these intentions, the sacrament would not take place. It would be considered null, hence the term *annulment*.

In regard to the first question, there may be several reasons why individuals do not come to the sacrament freely and without reservation. They may lack the mental capacity, due to a drug addiction or other problem; they may have placed conditions on their consent—for example, telling friends that they would not be bound to the marriage unless their spouse gave up a certain behavior or habit. Concerning the second question, if either individual held the belief that the marriage was not for life, the marriage might be annulled for that reason; if one of them was marrying for some other reason other than love and honor of the spouse, such as improved immigration status, that too might be grounds for annulment. The third question requires couples to be open to God's gift of children: if at the time of consent an individual intends not to have children with his spouse, he has positively excluded part of the meaning of Christian marriage, thereby potentially nullifying his consent.

Another potential reason for an invalid marriage and thus the granting of an annulment is called *defect of form*: this refers to a Catholic being married outside of the laws of the Catholic Church, such as before a judge or before a minister of a different denomination without a dispensation. Catholics are bound to follow

Church laws about the form of marriage in order for it to be valid (CIC 1108).

Some critics say the Church is being hypocritical when it says marriage is indissoluble but still allows for annulments: that annulments are just "divorce, Catholic-style." But nothing could be further from the truth. Divorce breaks (or attempts to break) a marital union; an annulment doesn't break a marital union but reasonably concludes that none existed in the first place.

There are two scenarios in which persons may be married, then civilly divorce and enter into a Catholic marriage while their ex-spouse is still alive. The first is called the *Pauline Privilege*, based on a situation that St. Paul describes in 1 Corinthians 7:10–15. In a marriage between two unbaptized persons, the bond is *natural* rather than the *supernatural* bond of the sacrament of matrimony. If one of the spouses becomes a Christian after marrying, and if the marriage ends in a civil divorce, the Christian may be free to enter into a sacramental union with another Christian. A similar circumstance called the *Petrine Privilege* (or *Privilege of the Faith*, or *Favor of the Faith*) refers to a marriage between a baptized person and an unbaptized person. If the marriage ends in civil divorce, the Christian may petition to be free to marry a Christian. (It is called Petrine Privilege because the permission must come from the successor of St. Peter, the pope, whereas the Pauline Privilege may be granted by the diocesan bishop.) In both cases the sacramental marriage supersedes the civil one; the supernatural is greater than the natural. This is why a purely natural marriage is ordinarily indissoluble but not absolutely so.

## 20. What are some ways I can make the sacraments more effective in my life?

"The sacraments not only presuppose faith, but with word and ritual elements they nourish, strengthen, and express it" (*Compendium* 228). Just as artists strengthen and express their ability by creating art and athletes strengthen and express their ability by participating in sports, so do Catholics—on a deeper and more vital level—strengthen and express their faith by participating in the sacraments. If we're Catholics who are serious about keeping God as the center of our lives, focusing on the sacraments is a simple way to do it; or, rather, a way that is simple in concept, but challenging in the secular culture we live in.

"The Eucharist is the source and summit of the Christian life. The other sacraments, and indeed all ecclesiastical ministries and works of the apostolate, are bound up with the Eucharist and are oriented toward it" (CCC 1324). In important matters such as physical health, we realize that daily attention is necessary. If we only concern ourselves with physical health once a year before our annual physical, we're not going to benefit much from the appointment. Likewise, if we concern ourselves with the Eucharist only during Sunday Mass, we're missing out on many of the spiritual benefits we could be receiving. Here are a few ways you can go beyond the bare minimum to reach a higher level of appreciation for, and benefit from, the Eucharist:

- If at all possible, go to Mass on Sunday morning rather than Saturday evening. The idea of going to Mass on Saturday in order *to get it out of the way* is dreadful.

- After Mass, either individually in prayer or in conversation as a family, find one aspect of the sermon that was inspirational or informative. It is easy to criticize sermons as being too long or too boring, but the purpose of sermons is not to entertain, and not every priest or deacon is going to be a gifted speaker. St. Teresa of Avila said that she gained something from every sermon she ever heard. Even if only one sentence was beneficial, focus on that as the one God wanted you to hear that day.

- Families with children involved in organized sports should prayerfully consider whether to stop participation on Sundays. It is not inherently sinful to play in sports leagues on Sundays, but at the same time it is the Lord's Day, and it is difficult to justify having the day regularly revolve around sports leagues rather than focus on God.

- For the same reason, avoid making Sunday a day to get caught up on shopping, household chores, or yard work.

- What *should* be done on Sunday? In addition to Mass, good ways to keep holy the Sabbath are spending time as a family, whether making a meal, doing outdoor activities, or taking a day trip; visiting relatives, especially the older ones; spending some time in prayer or spiritual reading.

- If possible, attend weekday Mass, and/or spend time at an adoration chapel, whether daily, once a week, or once a month.

There is a traditional but nearly forgotten practice called *spiritual communion*, of which the Catechism of Trent explains: "They are those who, inflamed with a lively faith which works by charity, partake in wish and desire of that celestial bread offered to them, from which they receive, if not entire, at least very great fruit." Those who go to Mass but do not receive Holy Communion due to being in a state of sin (or another reason, such as not fasting for an hour before) can and should ask God's forgiveness for their sins, and ask him to give the grace that they would have received had they been able to receive the Eucharist worthily. Rather than hardening themselves further by committing a serious sin, they are opening themselves to God's grace by their humble request. Similarly, those who are prevented from attending Mass because of poor health or other physical limitations may also benefit greatly from making a spiritual communion as part of their daily prayer life.

In regard to the other sacraments, going to confession every month or even every week can be life changing. In order to increase appreciation of baptism and confirmation, it is a great practice to attend when someone is receiving these sacraments. Going to the Mass of ordination of priests and deacons is always inspiring for the laity as well as the clergy. Similarly, visiting a convent or monastery chapel, or—even better—going when someone is making religious vows, is a good way to enliven your own faith commitment. Finally, in order to more effectively receive the sacraments, the Church recommends frequent use of sacramentals, such as holy water, the rosary and other chaplets, and blessings: "By them men are disposed to receive the chief effect of the sacraments, and various occasions in life are rendered holy" (CCC 1667).

## About the Author

Fr. Mike Driscoll is a priest of the Diocese of Peoria, Illinois. He was ordained in 1992, has been pastor of several parishes, and is currently serving as chaplain of St. Elizabeth's Medical Center in Ottawa, Illinois. He has a B.A. in economics from the University of Illinois, an M.A. in moral theology from Mount St. Mary's Seminary, and a Ph.D. in counselor education and supervision from Regent University. His book, *Demons, Deliverance, and Discernment*, is published by Catholic Answers Press. He can be contacted through his website: peterinchains.org.

# Endnotes

1 http://www.ncregister.com/site/article/vatican_no_change_possible_on_communion_wafers.

2 "The sharing in the divine nature given to men through the grace of Christ bears a certain likeness to the origin, development, and nourishing of natural life. The faithful are born anew by baptism, strengthened by the sacrament of confirmation, and receive in the Eucharist the food of eternal life" (Pope Blessed Paul VI, *Divinae consortium naturae*: AAS 63 (1971) 657).

3 The early Christian writer Origen, for example, observed in A.D. 244 that "according to the usage of the Church, baptism is given even to infants" (*Homilies on Leviticus* 8:3:11).

4 *General Instruction of the Roman Missal* 73. There is no place in the offertory procession for other symbolic objects to be brought forward, as is sometimes illicitly done at special-event liturgies such as those for graduations, funerals, etc.

5 GIRM 24.

6 Prummer, Dominic M. *Handbook of Moral Theology*, (Fort Collins: Roman Catholic Books, 1957), 280.

7 Catechism of Pope St. Pius X, Sacrament of Extreme Unction.

8 The final word on the subject is "The Church has no authority whatsoever to confer priestly ordination on women and that this judgment is to be definitively held by all the Church's faithful" (John Paul II, *Ordinatio Sacerdotalis*, 1994).

9 Any valid marriage between two baptized persons is sacramental; but even natural (non-sacramental) marriages, when valid, have the ordinary character of indissolubility.